May
400 Year Anniversary
1620 - 2020

Creative Advisor; Andrew J. MacLachlan

Cover Creator & Illustrator; Bonnie S. MacLachlan © 2019
all rights reserved

Editor; Susan Sweet MacLachlan

ISBN: 9781085830324

BookN.it Publications
BookNitPublications.com
BookNitPublications@iCloud.com
Griswold, Ct

John Alden

Mayflower Passenger
1620

Quick Reference Guide

Dedications

This notebook is dedicated to my family and all
the families that risked their lives to travel
to America, in search of a better life.

If You are a beginner or professional Genealogist
Mayflower Descendant, or simply enjoy family history
and want a special place to keep track of your notes
or research, then this is the notebook for you!

#NoteBooksThatTravel

The Mayflower Compact

(Modern Version)

IN THE NAME OF GOD, AMEN. We, whose names are underwritten, the Loyal Subjects of our dread Sovereign Lord King James, by the Grace of God, of Great Britain, France, and Ireland, King, Defender of the Faith, etc.,

Having undertaken for the Glory of God, and Advancement of the Christian Faith, and the Honour of our King and Country, a Voyage to plant the first Colony in the northern Parts of Virginia; Do by these Presents, solemnly and mutually, in the Presence of God and one another, covenant and combine our-selves together into a civil Body Politick, for our better Ordering and Preservation, and Furtherance of the Ends aforesaid: And by Virtue hereof do enact, constitute, and frame, such just and equal Laws, Ordinances, Acts, Constitutions, and Officers, from time to time, as shall be thought most meet and convenient for the general Good of the Colony unto which we promise all due Submission and Obedience.

IN WITNESS whereof we have here-unto sub-scribed our names at Cape-Cod the eleventh of November, in the Reign of our Sovereign Lord King James, of England, France, and Ireland, the eighteenth, and of Scotland the fifty-fourth, Anno Domini; 1620.

John Carver	William White	Edward Fuller	Gilbert Winslow
William Bradford	Richard Warren	John Turner	Edmond Margeson
Edward Winslow	John Howland	Francis Eaton	Peter Brown
William Brewster	Stephen Hopkins	James Chilton	Richard Britteridge
Isaac Allerton	Edward Tilly	John Crackston	George Soule
Myles Standish	John Tilly	John Billington	Richard Clarke
John Alden	Francis Cooke	Moses Fletcher	Richard Gardiner
Samuel Fuller	Thomas Rogers	John Goodman	John Allerton
Christopher Martin	Thomas Tinker	Degory Priest	Thomas English
William Mullins	John Rigdale	Thomas Williams	Edward Doty
			Edward Leister

The original document has been lost, so the exact wording is uncertain. Historic documents differ slightly in capitalization, spelling, punctuation and wording. The signers names differ in spelling from source to source.

400 Anniversary 1620 - 2020

Mayflower Voyage

Mayflower Voyage

2

3

4

Mayflower Voyage

5

6

Mayflower Voyage

Mayflower Voyage

Made in United States
North Haven, CT
11 July 2025

70582551R00068